I Name Him Me: Selected Poems of Ma Yan
Copyright © Wei Yuan, Estate of Ma Yan, 2021
Translation Copyright © Stephen Nashef, 2021
Translator's Note Copyright © Stephen Nashef, 2021

Some of these translated poems have appeared in
Michigan Quarterly Review and *Enclave*.

ISBN 978-1-946433-74-9
First edition, first printing, 2021

Ugly Duckling Presse
The Old American Can Factory
232 Third Street #E-303
Brooklyn, NY 11215
www.uglyducklingpresse.org

Distributed in the USA by SPD / Small Press Distribution
Distributed in the UK by Inpress Books

Edited by Sarah Lawson, chuck kuan, and Michael Newton
Design and typesetting by chuck kuan
Typeset in FreightText Pro, Authentic Sans, DFSong, DFKai, and DFHei
Cover typeset in Clifton, Genwan Mincho, and DFRareBook-Magnolia
Covers printed at Ugly Duckling Presse and Hodgins Engraving Co.
Books printed and bound at McNaughton & Gunn

The publication of this book was made possible, in part, by a grant from the National Endowment for the Arts, and by the continued support of the New York State Council on the Arts with the support of Governor Andrew M. Cuomo and the New York State Legislature. This project is supported by the Robert Rauschenberg Foundation.

UGLY DUCKLING PRESSE

I name him me

SELECTED POEMS OF
MA YAN

TRANSLATED BY STEPHEN NASHEF

TABLE OF CONTENTS

Rite of Passage	15
The Self's Art of Illusion	21
Suffering Does Not Destroy What Makes Suffering Possible	23
Saxifrage	25
With a Desire for Something	27
This Warmth Has No Source	29
A Sweltering Dinner in July	31
Dissection Class	35
Jokes, Irony, Mockery, and Deeper Significances	37
Study	39
I Respect Your Complexity	41
To Everyone's Demons and Angels	43
The Love of Little Girls	47
To the Walker by the Lake	51
Fine Snow	53
The World Rains a Night	57
Looking at the Lake From a Hill	61
Knocking Persimmons in Autumn	63
After the Rain	65
Cherry	67
That Tiny Door	69
The Person Playing Fiddle in the Snow	71

Murder	73
Sunday, I Sit on Glass	77
Stranger	79
The Dancing Bohemian Woman	81
Uncursed Salomé	83
Bus Chronicle	87
Yes, I Must Die	89
The Storm Is Coming	93
Sixth of July (Happiness Requires Concealment)	95
The Year Bacterium Was Born	97
Old Robot	99
Flirting (Teasing Out Feeling)	101
Just Take It Easy	105
He Falls in Love with Someone and Closes His Eyes in the Dark	107
Chengdu Nights	109
A Teahouse on a Rainy Day (or Lion Rock)	111
The Paintings Are All More or Less Disingenuous	113
Extravaganza	115
Love Poem	119
Dusk in April	121
Small Is Small	123
Smooth Talker	127
Television	129
We Have a Kitchen with All the Lights Blazing	131

A Gray Attic Houses Us	133
Wildlife Park	137
Fragrant Mountain	139
We Boarded the Rollercoaster and Flew into the Future	141
Acknowledgments	145
Translator's Note	147
End Notes	155

成人仪式

一

暂时,我还不能回到去年
不能回到和某人以及另一个某人
喝酒的晚上,我想,六月
妖娆的时节,汗水打湿的少年

从东直门到西单,一些简单的地名
甚至不能构成一种象征,还没有
触碰到的痛楚,和没有来得及的腐朽生活

忽然被一些雨水淋到了
皮肤最表层的点状晕染片
散开,融化了,泛滥了的抒情

从南到北,我遭遇到一生中最多的陌生人
陌生化的手指抚摩了最陌生的人
被晨光照亮的夜晚,黑暗终于变得
清晰,终于还没有这样接近过黑暗

二

某一年,具体的年份
不便说明
具体的人物,任何事件以及主人公
都不便由我,此刻
一个残忍的女人,来说明
残忍的季节
充斥着我的岁月

RITE OF PASSAGE

ONE
for now, I can't go back to last year
I can't go back to that evening of drinks
with somebody and somebody else, I miss it, June's
witching hour, youth wet with sweat

from Dongzhimen to Xidan, a few simple place-names
that won't even amount to a symbol, anguish
yet to be broached, decadence there is no longer time for

suddenly I am soaked in rain
inkblots on the skin's surface
dispersing, molten, an effusion of lyric

from the South to the North, I met more strangers than ever before
strange fingers ran over the strangest person
night lit by morning, the dark at last became
clear, at last, the closest I've been to the dark

TWO
some year, exactly which
I can't say
those involved, the events and their protagonists
it is not for me, a now
ruthless woman, to describe
the ruthless seasons
have flooded my years in the world

在浑浊的一个瞬间
一个只剩下瞬间的人
只能是女人

他,或者是他们
落泪,或者仅仅是一个街心花园

路灯光下诉说的女人
大概,真的,并不是

我,用更虚构的句子以及词语
表达,举杯,说
喝酒,她于是喝下了酒
我递一支烟
于是吸烟,我残酷的泪水

像男人那样滑落的时候
他,或许会拍打我的背脊
(性感的,微妙的,光滑的)

辛酸地,倾吐一些秘密
一些简单的
少年的伤感
而那些在模棱两可中

碰撞的,可以
命名为爱情
戏剧化的转变,忽然间

within the mud of a second
someone with only a second to spare
can only be a woman

he, or is it they,
cry, or is it only a garden in the middle of a roundabout

the woman telling stories in the lamppost light is
approximately, genuinely, not at all

me, using made-up words and phrases
to express, to toast, to say
let's drink, and so she drinks
I pass her a cigarette
and so she smokes, when my merciless tears

slide down like a man's
maybe he'll tap me on the back
(sexy, subtle, smooth)

bitterly spitting out secrets
some simple
youthful sentiments
and those things inside ambiguity

that collide can
be named love
dramatized transformations that fall

掉下来，猝不及防
展开，展开……直到

一点一点翻开，散落
看见无数的爱情在天空飞舞
不得不歌唱，不得不随之
即使，也不能再说什么
再继续沉默，或者就是这样
这样，飞舞着，如同命令

或者，一个命名

all of a sudden, caught off guard
unfolding, unfolding... until

they open up, bit by bit, raining down
countless loves seen dancing in the sky
you can't not sing, not go with it
and if there is nothing left to say
remain silent, maybe this is the way,
like this, dancing, as though commanded

or named

自我的幻觉术

一

太阳闪光，照在岩石和金属上。
只是等。等就是含义。逝者如斯夫，
有智慧的人在写字，留下暗示：
世界必有出口，你必有脱身的时刻。
你从海边来，带来咸腥的气味和光，
带来死，带来重生和绝望。
我复制你，翻转里外，
找出密码，等候重来。

二

细腰蜂正在经营它的巢穴，
黑色的脚上矗立着针头。
每背叛一次，就有一粒毒药
顺着喉管滑到岩石底部。
我策划着谋反和叛乱，
策划着如何挣扎着逃跑，
如何与你为敌，以便归降为
你的女奴。细腰蜂在它的巢穴里，
不知道我的阴谋，正如你
在睡眠中，不知我计划
周密，步步为营，正在策反
你的营地，这里处处流淌着蜜，
谁比我更爱你黑色的甜美。

THE SELF'S ART OF ILLUSION

ONE

The sun shines, gleaming on metal and rock.
Just waiting. Waiting is meaning. It passeth like this,
wise people are writing, leaving behind clues:
the world must have a way out, and you a good moment to leave.
You come from the coast bringing sea-smell and light.
You bring death, bring rebirth and despair.
I make a copy of you, turn you inside out,
find the password, await your return.

TWO

The mason wasp is busy in its nest,
needles sticking from its inky legs.
For each betrayal a dose of poison
slides down its stinger into the depths of rock.
I am hatching mutiny, a coup,
means by which to struggle for escape,
to make an enemy of you and then surrender,
your slave girl once again. The wasp is in its nest
and does not know that I conspire—just like you,
sleeping, know nothing of my plan:
precise, each step considered, an insurrection
in your camp, where everything is flowing with honey.
Who loves your blackened sweetness more than I.

痛苦不会摧毁痛苦的可能性……

痛苦不会摧毁痛苦的可能性,生命不会消失自我的幻觉术。在一生的时间里,穿越过岩石缝隙里的贝类是潜藏的隐微的音乐,那是宏大的乐队在奏响,人们正从缝隙里行军去往伟大的未来。是的,光明将从最卑微处散发,所有最恶劣的气味是大战乱的征兆。我坐在垃圾堆上唱歌,唱一支关于塑料和火结婚的歌。这支歌将唱响至地底的孤独者升起。他升起时,无花果树将开花,贝壳将给出回环的路径,一切再次降临,并反复以至于无穷。是这样;他说:痛苦不会摧毁痛苦的可能性。

SUFFERING DOES NOT DESTROY WHAT MAKES SUFFERING POSSIBLE

Suffering does not destroy what makes suffering possible; life does not do away with the self's art of illusion. In the space of a life, the shellfish that pass through the cracks in the rock are a hidden, infinitesimal music, which a huge band is now playing, and the people march from the cracks toward a magnificent future. Yes, it is true, light will scatter from the lowliest of places, and all the ugliest of smells are omens of war, but I sit on the rubbish pile singing, singing a song about the marriage of plastic and fire, a song that will sing the recluse underground up to the surface. When he comes to the surface the flowerless fruit will bloom, the shells will offer a path that loops back, and everything once again will descend, repeating until infinity. Just like this, he says, suffering does not destroy what makes suffering possible.

虎耳草

虎耳草的精神,是战胜
献出我们时代的过度,以及不足
颂歌一部编年史

一个腥臭弥漫的明暗界限
一个皱巴巴,不再润滑的恶女人

把即将显灵的神圣天才
卷藏在虎耳草丛深处

当我们达到巅峰
那淡黄色的光源,珍贵的精液
将蒸发,留下:

可疑的白色斑点

SAXIFRAGE

the spirit of saxifrage is of triumph
over the excess, and lack, which forfeits our age
a song of praise to the annals

a pungent division between light and dark
a wrinkled-up, no-longer-moist, evil woman

that takes divine talent just as it is about to appear
and rolls it up in the depths of saxifrage

when we reach the peak
yellow origins of light, precious semen
will start to evaporate, leaving behind

dubious white spots

怀着一个欲念……

怀着一个欲念,我拼命
拍打你的背,然后伏在上面
哭起来。你佝偻着的身体
温热,传透进我的皮肤。
不,不是这个欲念让我哭。
我们抬起头竭力撕开双颚,
把圆圈样的白牙齿朝向空中。
而欲念并不会化作一道烟,
从我们口中腾空飞走。
毒药正在肚子里发酵,
谁也拿不走,也没有谁能够
擦掉身上发炎的赤红皮肉。

WITH A DESIRE FOR SOMETHING

With a desire for something, I throw myself into
patting your back, then slump on top
and begin to cry. Your stooped body
is warm, seeps into my skin.
But no, this isn't the desire that makes me cry.
We lift our heads and wrench open our jaws with all of our might
pointing our rounded teeth to the sky.
But desire will not transform into smoke
and soar in a column from our mouths.
The poison will sour in our stomachs,
no one can take it away, and no one can
rub away the swollen red skin on our bodies.

这温暖没有来由

这温暖没有来由。
叫那颗长在潮湿中,
表皮布满橙色斑点的
毒蕈临着水沼发抖。
沼泽里正在跳舞比赛!
招摇的水草也油油地
乱摆,谁都逃不了。
从来太阳不能光顾这里,
而它们发出自己的光,
腐熟的气息费力挣扎
想升腾起来,却只在
匍匐的灌木中穿行。

THIS WARMTH HAS NO SOURCE

This warmth has no source.
Make the orange-spotted toxic mushroom
grown from a seed in the wet
tremble by the swamp.
A dance competition is about to begin in the bog!
The reeds that sway also leisurely
disarrange, no one can escape.
This is a place the sun has not managed to visit;
they make their own light.
The air of the rotten strives to ascend
into the sky, but can only
worm its way through the low-lying shrub.

七月的一次炎热晚餐

她们坐着,两两相对
互相瞪视对面女子的鼻梁
以及鼻梁两侧的眼睛

没有人说喝酒

晚餐的过程是平和的
一锅鱼汤以及四份凉菜
金属的筷子在她们指间滑动
因为汗液,
益发地光滑了

准确地说,她们是一群不合格的女人:
她们抽烟,夜不归宿
甚至在背地里搞同性恋

此刻她们是纯洁的
餐巾纸握在左手
右手礼节性地慵懒着
空中选准了角度悬着

然后探向一片萝卜
或者未知的另一种优美
她们开始走神

四条腿已经相撞,依靠着
剩下四条在犹豫
一些音乐传来,于是沉默

A SWELTERING DINNER IN JULY

the four women sit, two on each side of the table
they stare at the nose opposite them
and the eyes on each side of the nose

no one mentions having a drink

the evening passes gently
a pot of fish soup and four sides
metal chopsticks slide between fingers
unusually slippery
because of the sweat

strictly speaking these women are not proper:
they smoke, are out all night
when the world's not looking they do things with women

but right now they are pure
tissues held in left hands
a languid right hand lifted politely
chooses its angle, hangs poised

then roots out a radish slice on the plate
or some other unknown delight
their attention begins to wander

four legs meet and rest on each other
the other four hesitate
music comes from somewhere, and so they are quiet

隔着桌子可以望到对面的
低胸装开口,和她的睫毛

她吹口哨
她说:看什么呢?

一碟菜没了,汤剩下了
她说,浪费
另一个人撇撇嘴

后来时间过去了
她们起身离开

很多条腿在众目睽睽下
领走了她们

from across the table they each see
the other's low neckline, her eyelashes

she whistles
she says: *what are you looking at?*

the sides are gone, some soup is left
she says: *what a waste*
another curls her lip

later when the time has come
they stand up to leave

under everyone's gaze a gang of legs
leads them out

解剖课

> 解剖床上的情人们,我向你们致意

凝固的赭石色肉糜色泽沉郁,
流淌向窗棂外的光亮。

孩子们正在弧型长廊下拍洋画,
瓦罐中的水越积越深,越积越冷。

下午时分,金鱼藻底浮起水泡
钟楼正投下阴郁的影子。

七里香、雨雾和淡蓝色的烟……
淡蓝色的烟飘过整个医学院。

踏朱红色地板"咚咚"作响,
解剖床上他们重叠着交合。

DISSECTION CLASS

Lovers on the dissection table, I send you my regards

The gloom of congealing hematitic mince
flows toward the light outside the window.

In the curved corridor kids take photos of oil paintings
as water caught in a pot gets deeper and colder with every drop.

In the afternoon, bubbles rise from beneath reeds
while the clock tower casts its dark shadow.

Orange jasmine, fog, and a pale blue smoke...
the pale blue smoke floats over the whole medical school.

A red floorboard creaks when stepped on.
They come together entwining on the dissection table.

玩笑、讽刺、嘲弄和更深刻的意义
    献给伟大的 C. Grabbe

在我的胸口汹涌的,不断喷涌而出的
不是乳汁,也不是激情,而是无法命名。
这些单数的人群,他们仅仅是他们。
犹豫着不能断定的,在廊街漫游。
这些人群中的人,在妓院外徘徊,颤抖
抱头痛哭幸福的消逝。污水里我生出
一个儿子,他的名字叫做"我"。
我要触摸我的光环,我要折断我的骨头。
没有一把匕首可以插入他。分开腿,抓住
儿子的头,把他拖出来,把他拉扯大。

JOKES, IRONY, MOCKERY, AND DEEPER SIGNIFICANCES
    for the great C. Grabbe

What surges in my chest, what keeps gushing out,
isn't milk, or passion either. It can't be named.
The singular crowds, they are only them.
Unsure what to do, they roam the alleyways.
The people inside the crowds pace outside the brothels.
   They tremble
and weep with their heads in their hands for the passing of joy.
   In the filth
I give birth to a son. I name him me.
I want to touch the halo that encircles me, I want to snap the
   bones inside.
No dagger can pierce him. I spread my legs and grab
my son's head, drag him out, stretch him out big.

学习
　　给颜峻

抓住这个脱口而出的词，
回想过去完美的时间，从来
恰当于理由，也不缺少完美的
解释。而一切贬义词都能被
赋予崭新的意思，应始终
善于把握尺度，和从头开始。
临风，但不招展，是一个
充满厌倦情绪的享乐主义者，
痴迷于尖刻的自我教育和
政治斗争的佝偻病人。怀念
与朋友们暴雨夜里饮酒的
时日，如今它们再也回不来。
亲爱的自由生活，亲爱的
冰凉、汗水、玩笑以及火焰。
保持婉约的风度，逢迎
陌生人时不动声色的娇嗔，
当迅疾的豪雨降临，则
挥动残暴的盾牌抵毁自己。
"那甚至不如一只无花果！"

STUDY
    to Yan Jun

Grab hold of the word that bursts out
and think back to the perfect time, always
germane to your purpose, never lacking a perfect
explanation. All negative terms can be
assigned a new meaning, at all times
keep a sense of proportion and start from the beginning.
To face the wind and not flutter is to be
a hedonist bored out of her mind, a cripple
obsessed with relentless self-education
and political struggle. Cherish the times
you got drunk with your friends
on nights wracked with storms. They're not coming back.
My dear unfettered life, my dear moments
of cold and sweat, of jokes and flames.
Maintain a graceful composure, when meeting
with strangers, flirt without tremor
in your voice or your face. When the tempest approaches,
brandish your belligerent shield in self-defamation.
"And yet no better than a common fig!"

我尊重你的复杂

我尊重你的复杂,一切
都合乎情理——再搞些个
愁苦的镜头,也无济于事。
好几年了,我趴在阳台沿上
偷看你摆弄人性,或捏造
一个银灰色飞行器模型。
出乎意料!我竟迅速长成,
直接进入中年的沉静与执着。
我迷恋你,数十年如一日:
复杂,如密密麻麻的格子
为了互相混淆,而面目相似。
每个毛孔里,藏一个魔鬼,
各不相同。每秒钟制造
一个新的欲望。冰冷僵硬
如水泥所造尸体,你是
完美无生命体。而我则是
简单,你看我如此简单,
作为你的反对。当我说出
"正确"就意味着结束。
此刻,万物凋零正是时候。

I RESPECT YOUR COMPLEXITY

I respect your complexity, everything
makes sense—film another few
angsty scenes, it won't make any difference.
For years I lay face down and peered over the side of the balcony
to see you messing around with human nature, or cooking up
a model for some silver flying machine.
What next! I grew up fast in the end,
straight into the quiet obstinacy of middle age.
I was fascinated with you, decades felt like a day:
complex, a densely packed grid
where each square only looks alike so that people get them confused.
A new monster hides in every pore,
each one different. Every second gives birth
to a brand new desire. You are icy stiff
like a corpse made of concrete,
a perfect lifeless form. Whereas I am just
simple, see how simple I am,
I am your opposition. When I say
"Correct," it signals the end
and right on time everything wilts.

献给每个人的魔鬼天使
为康赫,中国最伟大的小说家而作

所有虚构的事实,构成康赫

1
他是魔鬼,
他也是天使。

他没有出现过,
他从来就不会出现。

他只出现在对事实的描述中,
他远不止是事实。

因为我是上帝,
所以他将避开我。

2
今天晚上,他出现在酒的外部,
成为一具清瘦的皮囊。

也是今天,极度寒冷的半夜,
他将从清河走到电影学院。

而在知识的内页,他傲慢
鸣叫:"觚不觚。觚哉!觚哉!"

TO EVERYONE'S DEMONS AND ANGELS
for Kang He, China's greatest novelist

all the world's made-up facts make up Kang He

1
He is a demon
and also an angel.

He has never appeared
and will never appear.

He only appears in the description of facts
but he is not simply factual.

I am God,
so he will avoid me.

2
This evening he appeared on the outside of wine
and became all skin and bones.

On the same day he walked through icy midnight
from Qinghe to the Film Academy.

And from the pages of knowledge he chirps
with conceit, "That's no *gu*! Where's the *gu*? Where's the *gu*?"

3
"我看见了海,
他妈的!"

(我的愚蠢给我启示:
二不能出现为一)

3
"I saw the sea
for fuck's sake!"

(My foolishness gives me a sign:
two cannot appear as one.)

童女之恋
　　给小黄的情书

　　　　　"问题是没有什么是值得付出代价的。这个世界上没有任何一种生活是值得过的,这是你的意思吗?还是我在胡言乱语?"
　　　　　"这正是我想要的,多么好!"

她躺在我身边,
"我妒忌所有的,你爱过的
女人,所有的,
所有的……"

而她在那边抽泣,
没什么,
只是很想你,
很想你。

"我心里好难过啊!"
她竟然这样叫喊起来!

这时,
我张大嘴巴,拼命吃。
好像要把世界上所有难吃的东西
都吃到我一个人肚子里。

我一个人肚子里。
"这正是我要的,多么好!"

THE LOVE OF LITTLE GIRLS
a love letter for Huang

> *"The problem is that nothing is worth the price we pay for it. There is no life in this world that's worth living. Is this what you mean? Or am I missing the point?"*
> *"That's all that I wanted, how wonderful!"*

She lies beside me.
"I am jealous of them all, all the women
you've loved, all of them,
all of the…"

And she sits there sobbing.
It's nothing,
I just miss you,
I miss you.

"But it hurts!"
She actually shouts.

At this point
I open my mouth and eat with all of my might
as though I wanted to take all that's foul in this world
into my stomach.

Into my one single stomach.
"That's all that I wanted, how wonderful!"

是的,那是一个人所能达到的最高度。
我反复回味这句话,
他念着咒语。我反复回味着,
是的,我必须向她表明我的看法。

不会有人听到我怀孕的声音了。
她在电话里对我说:"不知道为什么,
窗户让我想到了末日。"

真的可能像他说的那样吗?
病症,已经越来越让我着迷。
这是你的意思吗?

"Life is sweet,
and...life is sweet."
这是一切的前提。
我们爬上天台之前,
并没有意识到暴风雨将要来临。
一切正在朝新的方向旋转。
亲爱的,我在岩石缝里给你写诗。

"我已百炼成钢",
这是多么好的事情。

Yes, this is the highest a person can reach.
I roll the sentence over my tongue again and again,
he's reciting spells, I roll it over again and again,
yes, I should let her know what I think.

No one will hear my pregnant voice anymore.
I hear her say through the phone, "I don't know why,
but the window makes me think of the end of the world."

Can it really be as she says?
I am drawn to the disease more and more every day.
Is this what you mean?

*"Life is sweet,
and... life is sweet."*
This is all we have for a premise.
Before we climbed onto the roof
we had no idea that a storm was on the horizon.
Everything is turning toward something new.
My love, I write you a poem from the cracks in the rock.

"I am steel hammered into shape a hundred times over."
This is a wonderful thing.

致湖边散步者
　　为田雨阳

其实，你并不经常散步
我们谈到你，在晚上
半小时的路程，她笑起来
经常，因头脑中的情景发笑
说不定，当时你正在湖边
我不能看见你散步的景象
即使在头脑中。非常好，
你说你很少去湖边，散步
"如果有一天再也不能……"
一个天真的、忧伤的问题
或者，接受这样一个想象
如果我再也不能去湖边散步
这意味着什么呢？除非是死亡
有时候，死亡仅意味着这一点变化
湖面上的雾，已经微凉的风
（现实本身总是比现实更冷）
现在，描述一次湖边的散步吧
早春的周末下午，乘公共汽车来到郊外
沿着引水渠渐渐接近湖边
几百米外，水鸟从枯草丛中飞起来
两个男孩用长柄网兜捞鱼
"阿姨"，他们这样叫我
手插在裤兜里，夹着肩膀
一对中年男女倚着栏杆，拥抱
杨树花穗偶尔飘落到脚边
在湖边，张望片刻，慢步返回

TO THE WALKER BY THE LAKE
   for Tian Yuyang

In fact you hardly ever go walking
we speak of you, in the evening
on the half-hour walk, she smiles
not rarely, a scene makes her laugh, in her mind
perhaps, just as you're by the lake
I cannot see the scene of you walking
even if it is in my mind. Wonderful
you say you hardly ever go to the lake to go walking
"If one day I am no longer able... "
A simple, sad question
let's consider this thought:
were I no longer able to go to the lake to go walking
what would it mean? Apart from death
sometimes death means only these slight deviations
the fog on the lake, the wind getting cold
(what's really real is always colder than reality).
Now let us describe a walk by the lake
an afternoon, a weekend, in early spring, a bus trip to the suburbs
skirting the canal approaching the lake
a few hundred meters away, ducks fly up from dried grass
two boys with nets are scooping out fish
Auntie, they call me
with their hands in their pockets, shoulder to shoulder
a couple, middle-aged, lean on a fence, they hug
poplar blossoms fall here and there by their feet
by the lake, we take in the scene, then walk back.

细雪

Eternity and a Day

穿树皮靴的人,
把我带到深邃的胡同里,
小鸭子胡同,鸭雏胡同,
鸭蛋胡同,哪一个更像真的?
我们在小鸭子胡同里找小偷。
这些坏蛋,他们骗我,
你要把他们找出来。

我要把他们找出来。
这城里天天有人跳楼,
我哥哥说他要"自刎",
他一边说一边笑。
他们一直跳,
从一栋跳到另一栋,
乘着雨夹雪的风,
趁着没有人抬头看,
他们滑翔。

我是坏人,
但现在不是。
现在我是楚楚可怜。
人人都应该站在我面前,
透过湿润的冷看我。
坏心眼在飞转。

这湿润的冷!
正在弥漫着不清晰的城。

FINE SNOW
Eternity and a Day

The man in bark boots
took me to the depths of the *hutongs*,
Little Duck Hutong, Duckling Hutong
Duck Egg Hutong—which one sounds more believable?
We are looking for thieves in Little Duck Hutong.
The bastards tricked me
and you're going to find them.

I'm going to find them.
Every day in this city someone jumps off of a building.
My brother says he wants to slit his own throat.
He says it with a smile.
They keep jumping
out of one building and into another
riding the sleet in the wind
and when no one's raising their head to look at the sky
they soar.

I can be a bad person
but now I am not.
Now I am delicate and charming.
Everyone ought to stand before me
and look at me through the damp cold.
Bad intentions fly back and forth.

This damp cold!
It's seeping through this blurred city.

穿树皮靴的人,
抽打着,抽打着。

这些坏人,穿过马路
在清寒中低着他们的头。

And the man in bark boots
is pummelling away.

The bad guys are crossing the street,
heads lowered in the chill.

世界下着一夜的雨……
　　为卓青

世界下着一夜的雨,
这寻常一夜——
有人在电视机前消磨着有益的人生,
有人在酒杯里沉没、浮起,
有人在欲望下捏碎懦弱、锻造自我。
这些并不仅仅是概念,
你会同意,世界必须归类。
我想着,仲春天气,园中的乔木,
水草,以及人在岸边舞蹈。
我们享受过的朗姆酒冰淇淋……
如果把生活中的伤痛
呈现给你,也许就有变数。
但也许不,他人的愈合与你无关。
我迟疑在那个仲春,
温暖而黑暗的聚会,啤酒,拥抱,
早晨的口红,照相机。
中关村。与爱过的人一起吃午饭。
犹太史。闷热的咖啡厅。
全部的生活细节正在涨潮……
唯一的一个晚上:
你爬山归来,刚刚度过一场危机。
你不是第一个,也不会是最后一个。
我坚信:
那一刻我与你同在。
那一夜的雨同样淋湿我。
你意味着不敢想象,
乡村上空的乌鸦是死亡的符号,

THE WORLD RAINS A NIGHT
   for Zhuo Qing

The world rains a night,
this ordinary night—
some spend precious lives in front of the telly,
some sink into booze, sink and then rise,
some crush their flaws beneath their desires, forge themselves anew.
These are not simply abstractions,
you would agree, the world must be categorized.
I think of weather mid-spring, tall trees in the garden,
the reeds and those who danced on the banks.
The rum ice cream we loved...
Let us take life's hurt. If I present you with this,
perhaps we will have a variable.
But perhaps not. The way others heal is separate from you.
Let me stay a while with mid-spring:
warm and dark parties, beer bottles and hugs,
the morning's lipstick, a camera.
Zhongguancun. Lunch with someone you once loved.
A history of Judaism. A stuffy café.
All of life's details, rising...
And the only evening:
you came down from the mountain having weathered a crisis.
You aren't the first and won't be the last.
Of one thing I'm sure:
that moment I was there with you.
That night I was wet from the same rain.
You now mean what cannot be imagined;
the crows flying over the village are symbols of death

但未必不祥。
此刻我只能缅怀那只温暖的我握过的手。
你成为众人分享的记忆,
而我此生的工作是对记忆的镌刻。

but not necessarily of bad things to come.
All that's left now is to recall a warm hand in my own.
You became a memory everyone could share
and my work in this life is to chisel at memory.

在小山上看湖

晚上八点,
我们四人在小山顶的露台上看湖。
她俩在我右侧,他在我后方,
松松散散地站着,互相呼应。半侧身子。
椅子在身后不远处。靠着栏杆,
一口一口抿菊花茶依稀的甜味。
稀疏的树冠围拢,湖面只一亩大小,
远一点是路灯。更远的公路上有汽车。
她说:"空气真好,感觉真好。"
我说:"是的,连工地打桩的声音
都显得不难听了。"
我们像情人一样沉默,
像看情人一样看湖。

LOOKING AT THE LAKE FROM A HILL

At eight in the evening,
the four of us look at the lake from a platform on top of a hill.
She and she are to my right, he is behind me,
here and there but in sync. Turned slightly away.
A chair somewhere not far behind. Leaning against the railing,
sipping the slight sweet of chrysanthemum tea.
The sparse treetops close in, the lake the size of a small field.
A bit further off there are lampposts; further still, cars on the main road.
She says, "The weather is lovely. This is lovely."
I say, "Yes. Even the noise
from the road work sounds nice."
We are silent like lovers
looking at the lake like a lover.

秋天打柿子

在秋天打柿子,缩着手脚爬上树桠,
眺望云雾里远处那些山,正在雾气中
磅礴。我的身躯无限壮大,蓬勃而出,
向潮湿的寒冷伸出臂膀,正在升起,
我无限的躯体,照耀金红的果实。
雨从空无中降落,清洗积年的尘土。
十七个人,在秋天打柿子,挥动
铁灰色胳膊,长臂竹竿敲响无声的
节奏,果实落在我无限空旷的躯体。

KNOCKING PERSIMMONS IN AUTUMN

Knocking persimmons in autumn, arms and legs tucked, scaling
the tree, looking out at the mountains nestled in clouds,
 tremendous
in the mist. My body is vast, boundless, it sprouts forth into
 the cold
trembling with life, stretches an arm into the wet and ascends,
my boundless body sets the bronze fruit alight.
Rain descends from nowhere, cleans years of accumulated dust.
Seventeen people knocking persimmons in autumn, waving
iron-grey arms. Long-limbed bamboo knocking a rhythm
 without sound.
Fruit falls upon the boundless expanse of my body.

雨后

记忆正在变得琐碎,更加琐碎。
连昨天的琐碎都难以达到了,
代词越来越多,渐进地。形容词,
表示相关,任何的事都有联系。

上个月,我遇到十个人。
他们占领我的想象力。我剔除,
而乏力,他们随便地占据我
缺乏个性的想象力。我宣布:

长句子,严肃的和沉重的,
并且反对概念,要轻盈和跳跃。
只一个晚上,一场去除闷热的雨,
我忽然忘记怎么找那条密径。

AFTER THE RAIN

My memories are becoming more and more scattered.
Even yesterday's scatter is now hard to take hold of.
Pronouns are amassing, advancing. Adjectives
expressing relations, everything is connected.

Last month I met ten people.
They conquered my imagination. I tried to weed them out
but lacked the strength. Without a second thought, they annexed
my imagination, its lack of distinguishing characteristics. I
   hereby declare:

Long sentences, solemn and heavy ones,
and opposed to great concepts, should be light on their feet.
In the space of an evening, as rain swept the damp heat away,
I somehow forgot the way to the secret passage.

樱桃

我听过痛苦的声音,
从那一刻我缓慢病变。
那是沉郁的哀求,
不带抱怨,也没有
幻想。痛苦就是直接。

而痛苦是没有力量进入,
是软弱,不敢顽固并沉默。
我不敢把手探入它的核心,
不敢挖出血淋淋的鬼。
眼望着谎言的清洁。

当时我哀哀地哭泣,
转过脸,以缺席
担演无知,人人如此。
这一切就在面前:
痛苦,或者空无。

今天,我吃一颗樱桃,
想起一个女人在我面前,
缓慢,忍耐尔后大声喘息,
她曾经,作为母亲,
放一颗糖樱桃在我嘴里。

我缓慢吞食这蜜样的
嫣红尸体。是如此的红,
像那针管中涌动的血,
又红如她脸颊上消失的
欲望——这迷人之食。

CHERRY

I heard the voice of suffering
and that's when the symptoms slowly began to set in.
It was a desolate plea
bringing neither complaints nor
illusions. Suffering is direct.

But suffering is not having the strength to enter,
it is frailty, a fear of insisting. It is quiet.
I wouldn't dare reach into its core
to pull out the ghost dripping with blood.
My eyes are on sanitary lies.

At the time I was miserable and wept.
I turned my head, dressed up absence
as ignorance. Everyone does this.
It all lies ahead:
suffering, or nothing.

Today I eat a cherry
and remember a woman before me,
languid, holding back, then the sound of catching one's breath.
She once was a mother
placing a glazed cherry into my mouth.

Slowly, I swallow the honeyed
crimson corpse. As red as
the blood that surges into the syringe,
as red as the desire that disappeared
from her cheeks—this charming sustenance.

细小的门

我曾经在三层楼高的地方
看见过,细小的门
它在操场的对面
一堵孤立的墙上,墙是灰白色
当时,我闻到肥皂的香气

回忆那道门的时候
我形容它,是寒冷的
对,是凛冽的肥皂的寒香

四年前,我又看到了它
在一个晚上,经过了短途的奔跑
我来到一间教室,在一个女孩子身上
我看到了它,细小的门
在她的身上有着针尖一样的芒刺

这门,似乎和恋爱无关
它是我个人的门
只出现在某一个瞬间
我正沉浸在酸楚中的时候
它出现了,它从来没有敞开过
现在那堵墙已经不在了
我甚至不能清楚地看见它
但很清楚,它一直在
这细小的门

THAT TINY DOOR

I saw from my place on the third floor
that tiny door
it was on the other side of the playing field
in a detached stretch of wall, a grey-white wall
as I stared I smelled soap

when I remember that door
I describe it as cold
yes freezing, with an icy soapy scent

four years ago, I saw it again
in the evening, after a short run
I came to a classroom and saw it
above a girl's body, the tiny door
covered in sharp spines over her body

this door seems to know nothing of love
it is a door for me and me only
it appears just for a moment
when I am in pain
it appears, but it has never opened
the wall is no longer there
and now I can't even see it clearly
but of one thing I'm sure, it is always there
that tiny door

雪地里拉琴的人

我设想过,在你家
楼下,你拉琴。
是一个寒冷的天气,
过路人口中哈出稀薄的白。
我就变作一只乌鸦,
从你头顶飞过去。
飞过去,你的琴声
生动起来,好像跳舞的
水晶拨动你的耳垂。
你跳起舞来,你的脚尖
踢踏着,沾染我的黑。
我们的黑,我们的白。
就连雪地上,也有我滴落的
红,你的鞋尖还在跳舞。

THE PERSON PLAYING FIDDLE IN THE SNOW

I never thought that on the street
by your house you'd be playing the fiddle.
It's freezing, puffs of frail white
emerging from the mouths of people crossing the road.
So I turn into a crow,
flying from the top of your head.
Flying away, the sound of your fiddle
gathers pace as though dancing
crystals were tickling your ears.
You begin dancing, your toes
tapping, staining my black,
our black and our white,
and now even the snow collects my drops
of red, your shoe-tips still dancing.

谋杀

作为高深莫测的事件之主人公
她这一次要站在山冈上
听见风吹过树枝的声音
（衣襟是可以翻飞的，
头发是可以随风飘散的）
妒忌像牙齿　透入血肉
太复杂了　全无头绪

高深莫测的事件
难道只能像悲剧？
像高冈上的她投身于深潭
痛苦是风景　是必须的要素
（无人配合　无法确定时间）
没有理由　是因为弱点
因为想要温暖

风波起于一件事的开端
选择清晨出门
一边走路　一边歌唱
悲剧开始　无数丑角上蹿下跳
（她不知消失在什么地方）
冬天的雪　夏天的鲤鱼
有人从湖中心浮起
有人捞到褪色的遗书

自然　如果要神色哀愁
应该在松树下　松针上
山冈上有风但没有翅膀

MURDER

protagonist in a mysterious incident
this time she will stand on the hill
and hear wind blowing through the branches
(lapels can flutter
hair can billow in the wind)
jealousy as teeth   sinking into flesh
it's complicated   there are no clues

surely a mysterious incident
cannot only end in tragedy?
like her on the hill plunging deep into the lagoon
suffering is scenery   a necessary element
(she came alone   when exactly it's impossible to say)
for no reason   because of weakness
because of wanting warmth

a storm swells from the start of an incident
choosing dawn to set out
singing   as she walks
the tragedy begins   hundreds of clowns jump up and down
(she disappears somewhere   no one knows where)
snow in winter   carp in summer
someone is floating in the middle of the lake
someone scoops up a fading suicide note

naturally   if you're going to look so glum
you should go beneath the pines   on pine needles
on the hill there is wind but no wings

飞不起来的天使不是天使
长发飘飘只是妒忌与恶意
（语无伦次的疯女人
这一次要念诗　念两首充满暗示的诗
没有诱惑没有乱伦）
不必有笑声　　不会有
事件发生在午间

铃声响起　很突然
不要戏剧化　不能破解的悬案
终于停了　猜到是谁？
不能有差错
非常关心这一点
（小紫红花开了　开得小孩子气）
后来也不能下雨　　一下雨就完了
一点转机都没有

往左拐　往右拐
山冈上没有路　没有办法
只能这样了
不能在光线暗的过道里狭路相逢
反正最后无法确定
（风还是停了　没有什么山冈）

an angel who cannot fly is no angel
fluttering long hair can only be envy and spite
(the hysterical woman
will read poetry this time   two highly suggestive poems
free of seduction or vice)
no need for laughter   incidents
don't happen at noon

a bell sounds   very suddenly
do not dramatize   an unsolvable case
it finally ends   have you worked out who it was?
there must be no slip-ups
be extra careful about that
(the small magenta flowers bloom   with their childish air)
afterwards it mustn't rain   if it rains it's all over
the course of events is set

turn left   turn right
the hill has no roads   there's nothing to be done
it can only be like this
no inevitable encounters on shadowy walkways
there's no way to be sure either way in the end
(the wind has stopped   there is no hill)

星期天,我坐在玻璃上……

光照到地板上,反射,扎进一小片皮肤。
热也能是痛。敌人潜伏着接近我小小的领地,
带来他们的冷和甜。是那样甜,竟然也
能是咸与涩。那些在白炽灯下脱下外衣的人,
那些脱下内衣的人,不知道自己在动作的一瞬
扭动了。细小的腰,狭窄的臀。他们身体的
一小抹肉色,一小撮黑色,和红。扩大着,
倾斜进茫茫的白昼。这白昼里的旅行,滚烫地
穿过物质,穿过严密的逻辑。星期天,我
坐在玻璃上,坐在无边的翅膀上……回味
胆怯的话,菲薄的热情。不能融化的,仍旧
坚硬;阴影也没有可能抹去它的锋利。即使,
被一个个光斑晃花了眼,即使交叉的裂缝
拨动了脆弱的耳膜,这伟大的情种也不敢
掉头而去。不敢在这正午作夜间的啜泣。

SUNDAY, I SIT ON GLASS

Light flashes on the floorboards, reflects, pierces a small patch of skin.
Warmth can also be pain. Enemies zero in under cover on my tiny domain
with their cold and their sweet. It is that kind of sweet, that turns out
to be salty and tart. The people who take off their coats in the lamplight,
the ones who take off their underwear, don't know as they move that for a moment
they shudder. Slender waists, narrow buttocks. On their bodies
small daubs of skin, small pinches of black, and red. They swell up
and lean into a vast day. This movement through day bubbles as it passes
through matter, through logic's watertight rules. Sunday,
I sit on glass, on a wing without edges... I think back
to words said while afraid and paper-thin passions. What won't melt
remains hard; shadows can't rub its corners away. Even if I am blinded
by each burst of light, even if the delicate film in my ears is pricked
by forked cracks, the great romantic won't be able to give in
and leave. Not during this outburst of tears in this noon
masquerading as night.

陌生人
　　给凌越

陌生人,你的电话经常响起。
你拿起天文数字,像击中一颗
硬而凉的台球,漫不经心地跳起来。
在夏天晚上的风里,你的长手指
摸着圆滑和湿润。当光线明亮起来,
你漫步在郊区的杂草边,吹口哨。
把双手插在裤兜里,仿佛一个
不想回家的乡村少年。穿过人群时,
你匆忙消失的影子是清凉的鱼。

STRANGER
    to Ling Yue

Stranger, your phone keeps ringing.
You pick up the astronomical number and, as if tapping
a cold, hard billiard ball, jump without thinking.
In the wind of a summer evening your long finger
touches the smooth and the moist. When it gets light
you stroll by the weeds in the suburbs and whistle.
You put your hands in your pockets like a country youth
with no desire to head home. As you pass through the crowds
your swift-vanishing shadow is a cool fish.

跳舞的波希米亚女人

他抓来新鲜的鹌鹑献给她,叫她
母亲,叫她女儿,叫她嫁给他。
她摆了摆手,"你的血还没洗干净,
小雏儿,等洗干净那天再来吧!"
水草丰美的山谷里,枣红色骏马
在休憩呢,一颗子弹打中了它屁股。
我的骑马郎!飞奔,我的骑马郎!
她的手不比洁白更洁白,她的血
不比产妇更污秽。眼睛望着那海岸,
有人就将在那里丧生。可还有数不清的
人呢,在往这边赶,在拼命地赶!
波希米亚女人用头巾把自己裹起来,
钻进丛林,那是灰色的小毛驴带着她。
情人一个一个死去,她挂着项链,
在阴湿地里"啪嗒啪嗒"跳起舞来。

THE DANCING BOHEMIAN WOMAN

He grabs a quail and presents it to her, says she's
his mother, says she's his daughter, says she will marry him.
She waves her hand, "Your blood hasn't been cleaned
little duckling. Come back once you've cleaned it!"
In the verdant valley, a fine plum-red steed
is resting when it gets shot in the arse.
My knight! Gallop away, my knight!
Her hand is not whiter than white, her blood
no more soiled than the woman in labor. Her eyes are trained
   on the coast
where someone is soon to perish, but who knows how many
others are heading this way, running for their lives!
The Bohemian woman wraps herself in her headscarf
and enters the forest on the gray back of a donkey.
Lovers die one by one, she is wearing a necklace,
and in that damp and dark place she breaks into a clattering dance.

不被诅咒的沙乐美

今天,不被诅咒的沙乐美
来到大街上(旁白:可怜
沙乐美不是公主了)
她的手袋里装着五厘米长的
磨砂小玻璃瓶(赞助商:瓶里是香水)

沙乐美没有桂林步辇
她也没有鞋(贴身侍女:鞋店大减价!)
巴比伦最佳形象代表打着赤脚
  (道具:香水在瓶里发酵了
要不要扔掉)

沙乐美买了一张电话卡
粘在玻璃墙上打国际长途
  (会计:她把国库偷空了)
著名的自由主义分子,
在押政治犯的贵族情人

沙乐美逛商店事件发生在
本世纪初的一个春天
公主身着民族服装
盛装出游美艳动人
一群不明来历的反对派闻讯赶到

"打倒沙乐美这个小妖精!"
"不达目的誓不罢休!"
"强烈要求和王后
  (某甲:就是那个老妖精)直接对话!"
导致少女沙乐美离家出走的原因不详

UNCURSED SALOMÉ

today uncursed Salomé
arrived on the streets (ASIDE: *Poor
old Salomé is no longer a princess*)
in her handbag a five-centimeter
frosted glass bottle (SPONSORS: *The bottle contains perfume*)

Salomé has no mulberry sedan
and she has no shoes (PERSONAL MAID: *There's a sale at the shoe shop!*)
the exemplar of Babylon stands in bare feet
(PROPS: *The perfume in the bottle has gone off,
time to throw it away*)

Salomé buys a phone card
sticks it to the glass and makes an international call
(ACCOUNTANT: *She made off with the treasury's every last penny*)
the famous libertarian
is holding the political prisoner's aristocratic lover hostage

the Salomé shopping incident took place
in a spring at the beginning of this century
the princess wore ethnic dress
dressed up for a day out and dazzling
when news came in of a mysterious group of dissenters

"Down with the young temptress Salomé!"
"We won't take no for an answer!"
"We demand a reception with
the queen consort!" (PERSON A: *i.e. the older temptress*)
the reason for young Salomé's escape is not known

国王和王后之间发生了激烈的争执
"可怜的小宝贝儿,摇滚乐害了她!"
"她离家出走不过是因为
你也看上了那个自由主义小白脸!"
"看上他的还有你!"

流亡的公主,高贵的公主
你的脚趾如同纯洁的白鸽
流浪的公主,尊贵的公主
你的脸庞好像初升的月亮

沙乐美朝电话亭外的等候者抛媚眼
愿意和我跳足尖舞吗?
我好像见过你,《花花公子》封面?
是五月花酒店(导演:贵族式的微笑!)
到小酒馆喝一杯吧,今天早点开张

可怜国王和王后在家里死去活来
沙乐美的情人趁机越狱
回到家乡去会老相好
国王和王后终于决心离婚
"都是月亮惹的祸呀,沙乐美!"

there was a serious dispute between the king and queen consort
"Poor little baby, ruined by rock music!"
"She only left home because
you fell for that dreamy young libertarian!"
"You fell for him too!"

outcast princess, noble princess
your toes as pure as doves
roaming princess, righteous princess
your face like night's first moon

Salomé throws a lush glance at the person outside the phone box
shall we dance *sur les pointes*?
I think I've seen you before—on the cover of *Playboy*?
at the Mayflower Hotel (DIRECTOR: *Aristocratic smile!*)
let's have a drink at the bar, today let's get started early

the poor old king and queen are at home and their wits' end
Salomé's lover uses the chance to escape from prison
he heads home to meet up with an old flame
the king and queen finally decide to divorce
"This was all the moon's doing, Salomé!"

公共汽车纪事

闷热,更热的是车厢后部
起伏的浪,我如此谨慎。
之前,抑郁症患者的前身
从南中国的裤兜里悄悄掏出
食指与拇指之间的钞票,避人眼目,
潜伏,正在接近伟大传统。

售票员收走湿润的钞票,两张。
在传统中,存在着"一"的可能性,
但有人说:"二"不能出现为"一"。
当时,它们依靠汗液黏着、紧贴。
喊号子的人此刻正经过窗外,
他们面无表情,并且不着一物。

热的振幅里,波荡的中心
正在人体内移动。没有
无谓的人物,这里正是拥挤的尽头。
身下,发动机还在创造新的人生,
此刻,抑郁症脚踏菲薄的地壳,
胸中涌起难以排遣的犹疑。

要用坚毅的嘴角抵抗源源不断的词语,
要穿过密不透风的人群。他们体内的热,
如同怀着炙烧的阴谋,迟钝地杵。
我粗暴起来,不再沉浸于想。
像冰,迅速穿透伟大传统的中心,
融化了。现在,同肮脏的土混合着。

BUS CHRONICLE

It's stifling, even hotter at the back of the bus
where waves rise and fall. I mind my step.
A long time ago, in a past life, the depressive
took a note between her thumb and forefinger
from South China's back pocket while no one was looking;
undercover and nearing the Great Tradition.

The conductor took the moist notes, two of them.
The possibility of One exists in the tradition,
but someone once said, Two cannot appear as One.
They stuck and clung through the sweat.
Singing workers are now passing the window,
their faces expressionless and unadorned.

The heart of the oscillator swings inside people's bodies
caught in the heat of its sweep. No one person
is superfluous; this is the limit of the squeeze.
Under their bodies the engine is still creating new lives
when depression places a foot on the Earth's meager crust
and a doubt that is hard to dispel erupts in the chest.

Face the torrent of words with a resolute smile
and push through the packed crowds. The heat in their bodies
is a smouldering conspiracy, dumbly stewing.
I become brusque, no longer sunk in my thoughts.
Like the ice coursing through the heart of the Great Tradition,
I melt. Now I mix into the dirt of the earth.

是的，我必死

那个夜晚，他们撞开了
最后一扇门，他站在那里。
他站在门后的火中，
缠着裹尸布。四十年，
他是穿裹尸布的人。

他穿神的战袍，
说一个字，
竖起一根手指。
"一"，永远不能
出现为"二"。

自从他浑身素白，
就开始结巴。
他们说他说不出的话，
他们嘲笑他。哦，
你这个顽固的蠢货。

他郁结于心，不能
砸烂一个物事。
不能把纸做的真理
捏碎，要把力气捏在手里。
他夜夜失眠。

岂是人能理解的
伤感，岂是你们所说的
那些软绵绵的词语。
他沉默寡言，渐渐
连神也不信了。

YES, I MUST DIE

That night they burst through
the final door and there he was
on the other side, standing in fire
and wrapped in a funeral shroud. For forty years
he has been the man in the funeral shroud.

He wears the battle fatigues of the gods,
says one word,
and lifts one finger.
One can never
appear as Two.

From the moment his body turns white
he begins to stammer.
They say what he can't,
they ridicule him. Oh,
you stubborn old fool.

He is pent up inside, unable to
destroy a solitary thing,
unable to tear papery truth
into pieces. He must save his strength.
Night after night he can't sleep.

This is no sentiment mankind can
comprehend, not with those
mushy words you all use.
He is utterly mute, slowly
disbelieving in God.

他一日更胜一日
显出衰老的情态。
记不住一件事,
算不清一笔账。总之,
这笔账谁也不来还。

而握着长矛的人
"嗬嗬"叫着,跳起圆圈舞。
他冰凉着,倒卧门后。
要拦腰碾断,否则
何苦在门后守这么长时日。

The passage of days
reveals his senescent spirit
He can't remember a thing
or settle a single debt. That is,
no one will repay him his debt.

Meanwhile the men clutching shields
holler and dance in a circle.
He is cold as ice, behind the door in a heap on the ground.
Snap his body in half—or who knows
what torment could endure for so long through that door.

暴雨将至

铁色的墙在转角处
分娩出一个女人。

她细长的双腿
如同交尾的蜻蜓
互相缠绕,
灼灼着绿色荧光。
清脆的高跟鞋
踩破相邻的水洼。

这一刻她走来,
我激动不已。

楼上,窗帘背后
患抑郁症的男子正热烈地
与自己做爱。爱,爱……
他呢喃着,她扭动着。

当她抬起盲目的眼睑,
千亿个碎片撞向彼此。

THE STORM IS COMING

The iron-colored wall spawns
a woman at its corner.

Her long slender legs
interweave like the tails
of dragonflies mating,
sparkling luminous green.
Crisp high heels
pierce neighboring puddles.

She's walking this way now,
I can barely contain myself.

Upstairs, behind a curtain
a depressed man is passionately
making love to himself. Love, love...
He murmurs, she wiggles.

When she lifts her blind eyes
a billion fragments collide.

七月六日(幸福需要遮掩)

在海上,一个人捉到鱼。
黄昏,象驮着他,
于是看见大的夕阳。
沉到水底的时候,
月亮正慢慢爬。

人群的影子正经过,
飞快地闪过红色。
岩石上坐着国王,
桶中的小人鱼。

芭蕉裸露在暗中,
老鼠吃她的根。
正在麻痹的隐秘,
睁开的牛眼睛,
电流入了腕动脉。

SIXTH OF JULY (HAPPINESS REQUIRES CONCEALMENT)

Out at sea someone catches a fish.
At dusk he rides an elephant
and sees the big setting sun.
When it sinks to the sea-bed
the moon slowly climbs.

Reflections of crowds pass
with swift flashes of red.
The king sits on the cliff,
a mermaid in a bucket.

A plantain tree is exposed in the dark,
rats gnaw at her roots.
Secrecy dropping its guard,
cow eyes open wide,
electricity shoots down veins in the wrist.

细菌生年

这个动作将多次回放,你被严重氧化的
头发正穿过燠热的风。我迷恋,是
凝固的热。此刻,字幕无疑应该闪现:
"2002年8月26日"。白晃晃的光斑,
在这个时代的表层,显得悲凉而色情。

三十分钟后,我将向西跋涉,从高大的
野莴笋丛边经过。这是多不可思议的事情:
它们试图撩我的裙子。你的情人在南美洲,
是乡村女教师,是兼职游击队员。

这微不足道的过程。十亿个分子的彩色圆环,
也是短短一个光年。漫长的,太漫长的。

THE YEAR BACTERIUM WAS BORN

The action will replay over and over, your critically oxidized
hair flying through the boiled wind. My obsession is
solidified heat. Now is the time for subtitles to appear:
"August 26, 2002." The lights glimmering
on the surface of our age seem both desolate and erotic.

Thirty minutes from now I will trek west, through the tall
milk thistle. Something inconceivable happens:
they try to lift up my skirt. Your lover is in South America.
She is a village teacher, a part-time guerrilla warrior.

This negligible process. The colorful rings of a billion molecules
are also but a short light year. Long, far too long.

旧机器人

  分赠伟棠、颜峻

"就让我容纳三分之一个宇宙"

"她已经旧了,
被用得太多,
应该给她上些机油。"

我说,没错。
我已经被用旧,
请给我一些机油。

对事情不再发议论,
在安静里继续安静。
她已经被用旧。

忽然想到海
并继续想,关于海;
有时候想到人。

OLD ROBOT
    to Wei Tang and Yan Jun

"Just let me hold a third of the universe"

"She's worn out,
overused.
She needs some oil."

I say, too right.
I have been worn out.
Please give me some oil.

No longer offering opinions,
still quiet in the quiet.
She has been worn out.

But then, just like that, she thinks of the sea,
and keeps thinking, about the sea,
and, sometimes, about people.

调情

第一回,是在纸上,我说
"调情"。他说,"愤怒"。

第一回之前,他说"调情",
我说,"哦,那是什么?"

那是什么,他没有回答,
去打篮球了。打篮球了!

在篮球场上,调情是
什么滋味?一只松鼠跑过去。

调情,反过来:谁调了谁的情?
一张纸寻找一个字。

一滴墨水寻找一支笔。我们避免
一张嘴巴,避免一条僻静之路。

反过来,"情调"根本不存在。
她们,她们在酒杯后面飞媚眼。

还有她,她在倒扣的铁锅下面
扭屁股扭腰扭脖子,"怎么样?怎么样?"

"玫瑰!你想采摘我的玫瑰?
可是我的玫瑰喜欢诘诡,喜欢嘲诙!"

FLIRTING (TEASING OUT FEELING)

The first time was on paper. I said,
"Flirt." He said, "Rage."

Before the first time, he said, "Flirt."
I said, "Oh, what's that?"

What it was he didn't say
but went off to play basketball. Basketball!

On the basketball court what does flirting
taste like? A squirrel runs past.

Teasing out feeling in reverse: who teased whose feeling out?
The page looks for a word.

A drop of ink looks for a pen. We steer clear
of a mouth, we steer clear of a secluded road.

Flirting in reverse: there is no feeling behind the tease.
The women throw glances from behind wine glasses.

And she's under the upturned pot
twitching her arse, "What do you think? What do you think?"

"A rose! Would you like to pluck my rose?
But my rose likes reductio ad absurdum, how drôle!"

你要采摘我的玫瑰!
又一只松鼠,跑过来。

调情在酒馆里。在出租车里,
他对准一个焦距,缩短这个焦距。

调情,在大江南北。在日据铁道旁,
他漫无目的,心思密如雨。

集体迸发吧!在今天,占领
这里和那里,不如哼一首歌。

不如一只松果,被剥开了,
露出营养不良的籽。

又怎么可能流下一滴腥咸的
生理盐水?一直在打转,打转。

他吞下了,再吞下了,那喉结
一直在翻动。怎么没有完……

You want to pluck my rose!
Another squirrel runs past.

Flirting in the bar. In the taxi
he adjusts his focus, brings it nearer.

Flirting all over China. By the railways built under Japanese occupation
he is utterly aimless, his thoughts dense like rain.

Let's set out en masse! These days, conquering
this place or that is less fun than humming a tune,

less fun than a pine cone, peeled to
expose its malnourished seed.

So why that salty drip, that acrid bodily
saline solution? Always rolling and rolling.

He swallows and swallows again, his throat
pulsing the whole time. How is it not over…

不妨随意一些

这句话经常有人说,渐渐
演变成当代生活的标语。
不妨随意,在筵席上
他们谈生意,搞钱。
我也不妨随意一些,
搞不到钱可以搞时间,
随意支配,时间。
一路溜达进城,酒吧,
看这句话还没贴上墙,
已经挂成嘴上的老腊肉。
油爆得很嘎!疲倦的少女
总要说几句怨恨的话。
她们后来当上了主妇,
麻将桌上发泄青春的怨恨,
顺便也要发泄一些钱。
点到即止的骗局我没兴趣,
我不把"随意"当标签。
要谨慎,开场白是这个样子;
到后来说些话,似是而非,
毫无价值,废话,把我们的
生活撑起来,好像鲸须
撑起老妖婆的裙子。
而我打算"吭哧吭哧"地
刨地,我总要刨出点什么。
我总能在沉默中说出些什么。

JUST TAKE IT EASY

People say this a lot, it's
the catchphrase of the day.
Just take it easy at the meal
where they talk about business, making money.
I can take it easy too, why not?
I can't make money, but I can make time,
I portion it up as I please, my time.
I stroll right into town, to a bar
and see the catchphrase is not yet emblazoned on the wall
but it hangs off everyone's lips like old strips of cured meat.
They're greasy old buggers! Jaded girls
always have a few resentments to share.
Later they become housewives
and youth's resentments are poured out on the mahjong table
along with their cash.
I have no interest in the hoax of just touching the surface—
"take it easy" is not one of my labels.
Be careful of openings like this one;
whatever's said after cannot be trusted,
is utterly worthless, the nonsense that props up
our lives like the bones in a corset
prop the hag's evening dress.
My plan is to puff and to pant as I
scrape at the soil. I will always scrape something up.
In the silence I can always think of something to say.

他爱上一个人,在黑暗里闭上眼……

他爱上一个人,在黑暗里闭上眼。
就像失眠从来没有折磨过他一样,
沉浸在清醒里。发梢拂落耳垂边,
这种轻微的酥痒是他想要给她的。
脚趾甲尖顶住干燥的棉布,发出
丝绸一般的声音。响尾蛇的毒信
钻透她的鼓膜,是他游入了她的
大脑。殷红,网住了她。占据她
全部的白。她的,白。象牙的白。
膝盖,微微颤抖着。是被第一次
触摸到的身体,是第一次触摸到
身体的指尖,那背后是无边际的
阴影,他沦陷在此。他处处沦陷。
枕头是一架旧风琴,灌满了骨灰。

HE FALLS IN LOVE WITH SOMEONE AND CLOSES HIS EYES IN THE DARK

He falls in love with someone and closes his eyes in the dark. Like a man never plagued by insomnia he is sound awake. Hair-ends skimming earlobes: this is the tickling sensation he wants to give her. The dry cotton duvet is tented by toenails, silking sounds from the sheet. The rattlesnake: its toxic warning perforates her ear. It is him. Journeying into her brain, the red nets her, takes her all, all her white.   Her White.   Her ivory white. The light tremble of kneecaps. It is the body touched for the first time, it is the first fingernail to touch the body. Behind yawns a boundless shadow and he sinks into it. Everywhere he is sinking. The pillow is an old pipe organ. It is covered in funeral ash.

成都之夜

这是我们浪漫都市的夜景,
亲爱的,我带你游历一切。
你来得正当其时,下楼的瞬间
恰好捕捉一朵娇怯的眼风。
亲爱的,看这一切恰到好处。

我们互相搂抱,拿捏住尺寸,
再深一毫米也不能让我
对你更熟稔,在这里停下吧。
你应当四处流连,不妨
只在边缘抚摩,勿触中心。

而风雨之来也非我意愿。
每一次雨都让此地温情漫溢,
时不我与。我已经看到
你离开的景象。不止一次
我跟着奇怪的风跑起来。

当你来时,我正厌倦。
我们撒开手臂,却终究
垂下它们,你看这条阴沟。
亡命徒摁亮了霓虹灯
留下些透明的影子。

CHENGDU NIGHTS

This is what our romantic metropolis looks like at night,
my love, let me take you to all of its sights.
Your timing is perfect. As you descend the stairs
you catch a tender glance thrown your way.
My love, see how everything is just as it should be.

We hug, clinging tight to a sense of proportion.
I wouldn't know you any better if we got another
millimeter deep. Stop for a moment right here.
Feel free to linger all over; take your time,
feel out the edges, but stay clear of the center.

But this rain and wind is not what I wanted.
This place gets soppier with each spell of rain
and time is not on our side. I've seen the scene
of you leaving. It's not the first time
I've run after a peculiar wind.

When you do come I'm getting tired of it all.
We throw open our arms, but in the end
let them fall. See in the gutter
where neon lights switched on by some desperado
leave a few translucent streaks.

雨天的茶社(或者狮子山)
　　为凌越

我们的报纸上经常会有凶杀案的报导；
青年夫妇沉迷于麻将，他们的孩子，
三岁大，掉进窨井，为金黄的粪便淹没。
偶尔，住在垃圾堆后的老两口也会上报馆投诉。
而狮子山，树木葱郁，空气湿润，
似乎与这些无关。怎么会无关呢？也有报导，
青年男女，被勒死，叠在树荫里。
(不如我们也去做一回偷情的男女。)
被谁杀的呢？情敌，还是谋财害命者？
"我们的情敌"，你微笑着，带着自嘲，
无非是十年前街口的洗发妹，或者
一个长相清秀的木匠学徒，用刨子把我
层层剥开……我，只好毫不羞涩地横陈
在你面前。他们已经离开我们的城市。
不，是我们分别的城市——我陌生于你的；
而你甚至没打算熟悉我。阳光斜射过来。
倾斜开始发生的时候，你躲在太阳背面：
我，躲在你的影子里。影子比我预想的更大。
(我还有可能在影子里做了一个游戏。)
你强打起精神，我则怀抱不真实的慵懒。
是的，沉默来得太晚，诱惑早晚将会降临。
只是现在，光竟然照亮了我们。

A TEAHOUSE ON A RAINY DAY (OR LION ROCK)
    for Ling Yue

Our newspaper tells more tales of grizzly deaths:
Young married couple engrossed in game of mahjong unaware when child
of three years falls down manhole, is buried in shower of golden manure.
Sometimes the old couple by the scrapheap write complaints to the editor.
Lion Rock with its lush forests and damp air
seems to have nothing to do with any of this. But how can it not? Another report:
Young man and woman strangled to death and left in heap in the woods.
(Better yet, you and I should play illicit lovers and elope.)
Who killed them? A rival in love or murderous bandits?
"Our rivals in love," you say with a self-mocking smile.
Only the hair-washing girl ten years ago on the corner,
or would the exquisite young carpenter take a wood plane to me,
peel me layer by layer… I can only lay myself
without scruples before you. They have long left our city.
No, it is the city where we parted ways—I am a stranger to you
and you have no intention of getting to know me. The light shoots in
at an angle. As it begins to recline you leap behind the sun's back
and I jump into your shadow. The shadow is bigger than I thought.
(I might have even played a game here.)
You try to perk up while I sink into an exaggerated languor.
Yes, silence came too late. Temptation will arrive sooner or later.
It's just right now we have found ourselves caught in the light.

这些画或多或少地虚伪……

这些画或多或少地虚伪，它们挂在墙上，
如同在凝视我们。我们在沙发上做爱，
在椅子上互相抚摸。这些画一直凝视我们。
它们或多或少是虚伪的，它们不能够
伸出手阻止我们，不能够用火焰或者水
赶走我们。来，我们到大街上来，或
钻进绿化带。这些在室外打太极拳的衰老者
或多或少地虚伪，他们及时地患上白内障，
在坚硬的壳后面凝视我们。这些送牛奶的工人
穿过我们起伏的胸膛，而我们感到被强风
刮伤的摇晃。我们逃窜一样的姿态来到沼泽，
在墨绿的草丛中做爱。我们用指甲抠掉
龟裂的颜料表面。总之，他们或多或少地虚伪。
他们不能看到这一切，他们不能看我们做爱。

THE PAINTINGS ARE ALL MORE
OR LESS DISINGENUOUS

The paintings are all more or less disingenuous, hung on the wall
like they're staring at us. We're making love on the sofa,
touching each other on the furniture. The paintings keep staring.
They are all more or less disingenuous, unable to
reach out and stop us, unable to summon water or fire
to drive us away. Come, let's hit the streets, or
delve into the parks. The geriatrics doing t'ai chi
are all more or less disingenuous, with eyes on the brink of cataracts
staring at us behind their hard shells. The workers delivering milk
walk past our undulating chests, and we feel the lurch of being
scraped by the wind. We come to the marshlands in a pretense of panic
and make love in the reeds. We scratch off the craquelure
with our fingers. In short, they are all more or less disingenuous.
They cannot see all of this, they cannot see us make love.

盛事

盛事的定义取决于诗歌的方向和力量。通常理解,诗歌不能阻挡坦克,但最起码诗歌可以给予一些安慰和希望。所谓众人为之而义成。义也有刈的意思,这盛事在此刻和杀戮有关,但通过诗歌,也许变成了一件美好的事情,而不是残酷。诗歌的确还不能阻挡坦克,这是诗歌的局限,但诗歌试图阻挡坦克,这是诗歌的宽广。

一

傍晚的时候,我听见一些广告声正在舞动。
人们在咀嚼食物,电视发出噗嗤的油炸声,
那是油腻的鸡腿和翅膀,儿童喜欢的口味。
不,我不喜欢这些东西,不喜欢,请拿走。
我说了,是的,请拿走,我正在自我循环,
一升水是奢侈,更何况一升油,请拿走吧。
人们都在自我循环,我们的热量足够点燃
整个宇宙。整个宇宙都在燃烧,我是其中
一星火光,在和群星作普遍的飞翔和巡航。
而脱离了队伍的小行星,不打算独自寻回,
他要求被邀请,他要求被引到辉煌的门口。
傍晚的时候,他给出一只钟表,要对时间,
他不断发出请求,而他们在门里偷偷笑道:
这可怜的小行星竟不知焰火表演已经结束。

二

如何在几万只触手间飞行,是一门艰深的
学问,而我懂得一些。我善于引航,这是
艰深的本领,我懂得,自幼便如此。难道

EXTRAVAGANZA

The extravaganza derives its meaning from poetry: both its force and its orientation. Poetry, as commonly conceived, cannot stop tanks, but it is able to offer some comfort or hope. This is what the so-called masses call virtue. But virtue has another meaning: to slash. Here, the extravaganza is related to the massacre, but through poetry it can become something perhaps more beautiful than cruel. It is true, poetry still cannot stop tanks—this is the limit of poetry—but that poetry attempts to stop tanks is its reach.

ONE

In the evening I hear the sounds of commercials gyrating. People chewing on food, the TV sounds of oil sizzling. This is greasy fried chicken, the flavors kids love. No. I don't like these things. I don't. Take them away. You heard what I said. Take them away. I am currently self-circulating. A litre of water is a luxury, a litre of oil even more so. Take them away. Everyone is self-circulating, our heat enough to ignite the whole universe. The whole universe is burning, and here I am, a speck of a flame, floating and cruising like everything else with the clusters of stars, and having split from the asteroid ranks I do not intend to go back on my own. He requested an invite, to be led to the glittering door. He offered a clock in the evening. The time needs correcting. His requests carry on while those in the doorway smirk to themselves: *This poor asteroid does not even know that the spectacle of fire is already over.*

TWO

Flying between thousands of tentacles is a difficult skill. I know it reasonably well. I am a good pilot. It is a difficult art and I know it. I have since I was a child. Is this not terrifying hubris?

不是一种可怕的自大吗？"对于傲慢的人
我善于乔装。"都是可怕的自大，小行星
毕竟是小行星，在白巨星面前羞愧地闪烁。
但在几万只触手间飞行，我擅长。在它们
盲目的搜索中，穿越、翻跟斗，甚至挑衅
也是必要的动作，以使触手显得更像触手。
是的，触手，多么了不起，应当展开攻势，
我们是宇宙机器的配件，各自具备着使命。
小行星善于打结，但不在于自己，小行星
善于声嘶力竭，但不是自己。仅仅因为他
无法找到出发点，他只能不断地飞行向前，
而没有终点，终于等到触手不再延展那刻。

三

自从起飞以后，小行星就一直在翻腾，数万种
姿势都在刺向他。他也有数万种姿势刺向宇宙，
但从不施展，听说保留是小行星最主要的节目。
宇宙有最简单的逻辑，星体们都以爆炸为奉献，
爆炸们有着简单的逻辑和复杂的逻辑，纷飞的
是小小的喜悦、痛苦和无知。与世界和解的是
过后的宁静，很大的宁静，像曾经存在的海浪。

"When it comes to arrogant people I am good at disguise." This is all terrifying hubris. Asteroids, in the end, are just little planets, twinkling ashamed before the white giants. But flying between thousands of tentacles I can do very well. Through their blind groping I soar and I spin and I even provoke. It must be done, so the tentacles seem more like tentacles. Yes, the tentacles, they're not to be sniffed at; we must go on the offensive. We are the machine parts of the universe, each with our own little assignments. Asteroids are good at tying up knots but not in themselves. Asteroids are good at shouting themselves hoarse but cannot be themselves. He cannot find his point of departure so can only keep flying ahead with no end in sight, just until the tentacles stop stretching out.

THREE

Since taking off, the asteroid has been tumbling, all kinds of postures poking at him. He too has all kinds of postures to poke at the universe, but he's yet to demonstrate any; I've heard preservation is the asteroid's main entertainment. The universe's logic is simple: all celestial bodies can offer is
to explode. And explosions have a logic which is both simple and complex:
what scatters are small pieces of joy, ignorance, and pain. What reconciles
with the universe is the tranquillity after—a vast calm, a sea wave that once was.

情诗

熟悉决然割破了我。
我的心并非绝无情分,
此刻它正渐渐离开。
空气并未变得更稀薄,
的确,水是清澈的。
你的呼吸如此紧凑,
热烈而且清洁。
我告诉你我看见了海,
"海……是大的。"
你走,穿过人群,
对陌生者举起双手。
那一对掌心是清白的,
我很清楚这种爱。

LOVE POEM

I was decidedly slashed by our closeness.
It's not that that there's no affection inside me,
but at the moment it is in a process of gradual departure.
The air has not become thinner,
I mean even water is see-through.
Your breathing's so compact,
it is sunny and clean.
I tell you I saw the sea,
"The sea... is big."
You leave and enter the crowd
and lift both hands in the air at a stranger.
Those two palms are a pristine white.
I know full well this kind of love.

四月的黄昏

我还没有看过暮色中
这片土地,广漠的绿色
铺卷过地面,平坦,均匀。
紫色的暮霭,稀释着,
渐渐漫过整个平原……
散发出可疑的鲜明,
在即将倾泻的黑暗边缘,
闪烁着,发出幽光。
这景色说不上美,
一切陌生的色彩展露出来。
一瞬间,黑夜就来了。
我们被迅速裹进安全的无知。

DUSK IN APRIL

I've not seen this place before
at dusk, a bare stretch of green
unfurled—flat, creaseless—over the ground.
Purple evening haze—thinning—
slowly swallows the flat land...
suspiciously dazzling.
At the edge of a darkness on its way in
it sparkles, gives off a soft glare.
This sight is not what you'd call beautiful,
all foreign colors on display,
but then in a flash night arrives.
We are wrapped in the safety of ignorance.

小是小
献给阿才的情歌

> "我的恋人,我将没有声音再为你歌唱,
> 因为你刺伤了我的喉咙,连着我的心。"
> (巴布亚新几内亚民谣)

一、作为会飞的鸟
在世界的寓意,表面,
啊,你尖叫着!
多么像一只我叫不出名字的雀鸟:
你飞,但是你往往落下来。
一枝玫瑰也可以让你无所适从。
你停栖的树木,却往往让你厌倦;
甚至,你寻找的也不是玫瑰。
多少人为了玫瑰,这种传说中的植物
倾倒,于你的矫揉……
你掠过风平浪静的我们,
使我们惊诧于自己的惶惑。
这是一种陌生的感受,
而你,总是在陌生中一再熟悉起来。
犹如半斤基围虾,
就要爬出即将腐熟的巢穴。

二、作为悲伤而死的小女孩
这么说,你终于开始反抗了。
揪着衣角的手指,绞出你的汁液,
和你的轻蔑。而你几乎没有时间蔑视他们。
还没开始,我就猜到你必定缺席的眼泪。
你抽噎的样子根本比不上她们的斥责,

SMALL IS SMALL
a love song for Acai

> *"My love, I will soon have no voice left to sing for you*
> *Because you pierced my throat, and so my heart."*
> *Papua New Guinean Folk Song*

1. as a bird in flight
Where the world is allegory, its surface,
that's where you're screeching!
Like some bird I don't know the name of
you fly, and yet often land.
You can be baffled by roses, but
the branch you settle on usually bores you;
maybe a rose is not what you're after.
How many have toppled for roses, this fairy-tale
flower, into your charade...
You skim our windless waveless surface
and you startle us with our own incomprehension.
It is a strange feeling
and you keep familiarizing the strange.
Like half a pound of shrimp
trying to climb out of their festering nest.

2. as a girl dying of sadness
So you finally started to resist.
The fingers clutching the hem of your shirt wring out
your juice and disdain. You've barely the time to despise all these people.
It's hardly begun and I can already see your tears that will never arrive.
The sight of you crying is no match for their condemnation.

这时候我觉得你好像我的妹妹,
发生在我身上的,马上就将发生。
是谁?聪敏地掐断你的泪腺,
阻止了一场未遂的谋反?
你的眼睛从未如此明亮过,
那些烤鹅在我们转身的一刹那起飞了。
让我横穿马路去为你买一匣火柴吧,
如此,我们就是英雄的小姐妹。

三、作为传说中的花卉
我热恋于你的拖鞋,正如你反感我的猫。
你在我的幻想里瑟瑟发抖,
你的情人在你的水晶花瓶上方,
弹掉他第一百支烟的烟灰。
真的那么与众不同吗,你的幻想
其实只存在于我的幻想。
"我是一个坚定的唯物主义者!"
甚至,我幻想出了你的激昂。
我所摸不到的现实,你负责呈现;
当然,你有义务!他们把你放到领奖台上,
你四下张望,发现我是待发的奖品。
终于,你一步跨进自己的后半生,
留下我在台上放声大哭。

At times like this you're a little sister to me.
What happens to my body happens immediately
but who is it that's so quick to pinch your tear ducts?
Who is it foiling the treason before it begins?
Your eyes have never been as bright as they are now
and the roast geese took off the moment we turned around.
Let me cross the road and buy you some matches
so we can be the heroic little sisters.

3. as fairy-tale flowers
I fell in love with your slippers, just like you hated my cat.
The you I imagine is trembling
as your lover flicks the ash
of his hundredth cigarette over your crystal vase.
Are you really that different from everyone else?
Your fantasies only exist in my fantasies.
"I am a staunch materialist!"—I even
fantasize about your moments of passion.
It's up to you to reveal the reality I am unable to reach.
Of course, it's your job! When they put you on stage
you looked around and saw I was the prize waiting to be awarded.
At last you took a step into the rest of your life
and left me on stage bawling like a child.

中央空调

它们从梳子里爬出来
眼睛在老处女的窗户背后眨
眨巴,眨巴

一格,再一格
翻越了一个层次,再下来
就要升级成病毒了
水准一再地,将要提高

阴觑觑扑上面纱
(自杀可不行)
我们一再地探出身
其实,一缕小风
就能吹走你

(两秒后,将有南方来信)
在毒气室里,你对他谈女人
他却要和你谈圣经

七天,只有七天
要么把身体交给白衣人
要么现在就交钱,买断肠散

SMOOTH TALKER

they climb out of the comb
blinking their eyes outside an old virgin's window
blink, blink

one cell after another
across a whole floor, they descend
then upgrade to a virus
the water level will rise, time and again

they throw themselves furtively at the veil
(suicide is not an option)
time and again we put out our bodies
but in truth a breeze
could blow you away

(two seconds from now a letter from the South will arrive)
in the gas chamber you talk to him about women
but he wants to talk about the Bible

seven days, only seven days
either hand over your body to the people dressed in white
or pay up now, buy heart-shattering potion

电视

逆风爬行的蝴蝶,
在钢丝上蹒跚。
仲春的下午阳光,
蒙灰的道旁树,
互相打招呼。
这浓厚的北京,
浓郁的氧气味道,
电视信号偶然中断,
像正晌午的雷声。

TELEVISION

The butterflies climb against the wind,
they hobble on the cable.
Sunlight in mid-spring and
roadside trees smothered in dust
say hello to each other.
In this heavy Beijing,
the thick smell of oxygen,
the TV signal happens to cut out
like thunder at noon.

我们有灯火通明的厨房

我们有灯火通明的厨房,
我们有高大的柠檬色的墙。
你把我领上楼梯,我踮着脚尖,
把尖叫声刺向你头顶。其实,
你知道的,只要滴下一滴水
我就会被吓跑,风卷起几颗
灰尘就能叫我说不出话。
从啤酒内部的温热你看着我,
我们互相吸取着冻和坚硬。
这几天,你想到了爬山,
就爬到山顶上。从几千里外
刮来的风,忽然洞穿了我。
我是你灯火通明的厨房。

WE HAVE A KITCHEN WITH ALL THE LIGHTS BLAZING

We have a kitchen with all the lights blazing,
we have a great big lemon-colored wall.
You lead me up the stairs. I stand on my tiptoes
and aim a piercing scream into the top of your head.
But you know full well, one drop of water
will have me running away scared, a few
bits of dust in the wind and I can't say a word.
You look at me from the inner warmth of beer
as we absorb each other's hardness and ice.
A few days ago you thought of hiking a mountain
and then hiked to the top. From thousands of miles away
the wind blew right through me.
I am your kitchen with all the lights blazing.

一座灰色的小阁楼住着我们

一座灰色的小阁楼住着我们。
清晨,我们念悲伤的诗,因为
阳光正在蚕食这忙碌的城市,
属于我们的黑暗正在抛弃这片
干燥的土地。连河水也泛起
鳞光,连河水也抛弃我们。
我们躲在窗帘背后,把双手
用力地绞紧,绞紧……看,
嘴唇已经被咬得发白,阳光
快要照到我们身上。我们
念着悲伤的诗,紧闭上眼睛。

一座灰色的小阁楼住着我们。
正午,我们念痛苦的诗。痛苦
被锁在屋顶下面,因找不到
自己的影子而张大嘴巴,
缩成一团。我们互相厌憎,
似乎从来不是一对情人。
我和你,各自撕扯自己的
衣裳,各自钻进破旧的
安乐椅,在彼此的皮肤上
寻找肮脏的原由,却又不断
转过脸去,不愿彼此看见。

A GRAY ATTIC HOUSES US

A gray attic houses us.
In the morning we read sad poems because
sunlight is swallowing this bustling city.
The dark that is ours is renouncing this patch
of dry ground as we speak. Even the river is bursting
with glimmers of light, even the river renounces us.
We hide behind curtains, lace tight
our fingers, lace tight… Look,
our lips are clinched white beneath teeth, sunlight
is preparing to shine on our bodies. We
are reading sad poems, our eyes are shut tight.

A gray attic houses us.
At noon we read poems of suffering. Suffering
is locked in under the roof. It can't find
its own shadow so it opens its mouth
and curls into a ball. We detest one another
as though you and I had never been lovers.
We tear our own clothes
into pieces and nestle into worn-out
old armchairs and search for the causes of dirt
on each other's skin. But we keep
turning away, we don't want the other to see.

一座灰色小阁楼住着我们。
傍晚，我们念不成章法的诗。
身体已经疲惫，言语已经
失去意味。我们在安乐椅上
互相摇撼，我们不再相爱。
请为我买一罐糖浆，亲爱的，
请为我。不，亲爱的，请
不要这样。河水难道不仍在
窗下奔流吗？黑暗正袭来。
亲爱的，我们小小的糖罐
来不及看见自身，已经粉碎。

A gray attic houses us.
In the evening we read poorly-structured poems.
Our bodies are tired, language has lost
all of its flavor. We rock each other hard
on our armchairs. We no longer love each other.
Please buy me a jar of syrup, my darling,
Please, for me. No, darling, please
do not do that. Is the river not still rushing
outside the window? The dark is storming in.
My darling, it's too late for our little syrup jar
to take a look at itself, it has shattered.

动物乐园

他,颜色深蓝,像大地背面海水里的鲨鱼;
早晨的时候,他还是浅蓝,只是一只嫩贝壳。
到了夜间,他又成了透明的紫。穿过
他的紫,我看见,他没有心脏。那么——
温吞地跳着的、膨胀着的、收缩着的,
给出柔和的抛物线的,是什么呢?
横卧在他咽喉下的,不出声的那些。
他比线条还软地,穿过我,于是
我就湿润了。还有发出声音的那些,
使他就是蝙蝠,就是低声呼啸过的猛兽。
他在黑暗中蔓延,稀薄起来,更透明,
轻盈使他更加难以腾空。透过他,我看见
更浓重更黝黑的自身,正慢慢下沉。

WILDLIFE PARK

He is dark blue, a shark in the waters behind the earth's back.
In the morning his blue has paled, a tender mollusk,
but at night he turns that translucent purple again. I pass
through his purple and there's no heart to be seen. So what is it
that tepidly hops, swells and then shrinks, what is it
that gives off a gentle parabola? Those things
that lie under his throat making no sound?
Softer than an arc, he passes through me and so
I become wet. There are also the things that do make a sound,
that turn him into a bat, a deep-toned beast whistling past.
He spreads out in the dark, becomes meager, translucent,
his lightness keeps him from soaring. Through him
I see a denser blacker self, slowly sinking.

香山

人们出城乘车去往香山,沿路攀登着
漫长的路途,像水手登上有航向的海船,
一车摇晃的人享受拥挤,想象某种情绪,
忍受不尖锐的痛苦,像无怨言的牲口般。
是多么值得人沉醉的痛苦,多么轻微的
痛苦,多么不值得呼喊出的痛苦,是婴儿
所躺卧的摇篮,是晃动的国土,是地震。
也是一次毫无气味的风,和以往并无不同,
穿过盛满米饭的碗和碗之间,是不同的米饭,
是南方与北方的水稻步调一致呈现出尸体,
是温热的、无棱角的物体本质,是蔓延
于无规律布朗运动分子间不存在的空隙。
那差距理应存在,那想象中必然的区别
使感伤者能抱怨着,踢穿脚下的土地。
但并没有什么缝隙可使我们藏身,我们
隐身于人群,和他们一样。甚至可以说,
这其实是镜子里发生的自动粉碎事件。

FRAGRANT MOUNTAIN

Some people are taking a bus to Fragrant Mountain which climbs
a long road, the way a sailor boards a ship whose course has been set.
A jolting busful of people enjoying the squeeze as they imagine some feeling
and endure a soft suffering, like assenting animals drawing a plough.
It is the kind of suffering that is worth getting drunk in, a floating
suffering, a suffering for which there is no need to cry out. It is a child
in a cradle, the rumbling land of the nation, it is an earthquake.
It is a moment of wind without scent, no different to anything
that happened before, passing between bowls filled with rice, it is
a new kind of rice, the dead bodies dredged up all at once from the paddies
from the North to the South. It is the warm, edgeless object itself, it is
the non-existent rift extending between unruly Brownian particles.
But this division should exist, the distinction that fantasy needs
to make the sentimental complain and kick at the ground.
But no gulf can help us conceal our bodies, which we hide
in the crowd, for we and they are the same. It could even be said,
this is the event in the mirror that shatters itself.

我们乘坐过山车飞向未来

我们乘坐过山车飞向未来,
他和我的手里各捏着一张票,
那是飞向未来的小舢板,
起伏的波浪是我无畏的想象力。
乘坐我的想象力,他们尽情踩躏
这些无辜的女孩和男孩,
这些无辜的小狗和小猫。
在波浪之下,在波浪的下面
一直匍匐着衰弱的故事人,
他曾经是最伟大的创造者,
匍匐在最下面的飞得最高,
全是痛苦,全部都是痛苦。
那些与我耳语者,个个聪明无比,
他们说智慧来自痛苦,他们说:
来,给你智慧之路。
哦,每一个坐过山车的人
都是过山车建造厂的工人,
每一双手都充满智慧,是痛苦的
工艺匠。他们也制造不同的心灵,
这些心灵里孕育着奖励,
那些渴望奖励的人,那些最智慧的人,
他们总在沉默,不停地被从过山车上
推下去,在空中飘荡,在飘荡中,
我们接吻,就像那些恋人,
那些被压缩在词典册页中的爱情故事,
还有家庭,人间的互相拯救。
如果存在一个空间,漂浮着
无数列过山车,痛苦的过山车……

WE BOARDED THE ROLLERCOASTER AND FLEW INTO THE FUTURE

We board the rollercoaster and fly into the future,
tickets pinched in his and my hands,
a sampan flying into the future
on the bouncing waves of my fearless imagination.
When they board my imagination, they trample with glee
over innocent girls and boys,
over innocent cats and dogs.
Under the waves, in the waves' underneath
crawls the frail storyteller. He has been crawling all this time.
He was once a great creator.
Those who crawl the lowest fly the highest.
It is all suffering. Everything is suffering.
Each of those who whisper to me is the cleverest person I know,
they say wisdom comes from suffering. They say:
here, I give you the road to wisdom.
Huh. The people on the rollercoaster
are the factory workers who build it,
hands full of wisdom, artisans
of suffering. They build different souls,
each bearing the rewards it engenders.
All those people who thirst for reward, those wisest of people,
never say a thing, constantly being hurled off the sides
of the rollercoaster, fluttering in the air, and while fluttering,
we kiss, as if we were lovers.
The love stories squashed between the pages of dictionaries,
and family, people's way of rescuing each other.
If there were a space with infinite rollercoasters,
floating suffering rollercoasters...

ACKNOWLEDGMENTS

I began the work of translating Ma Yan's poems in 2017. It was the first time I decided to embark on a translation project of this size independently, based entirely on my own belief in the work. In the years that have followed I have continued to pick up newly printed versions of my translations and scrawl amendments in the margins, an endless process with which I am sure many translators, enamored with what they are translating and terrified of the possibility of failing to do it justice, are familiar. During this time I have benefited enormously from the emotional and intellectual guidance of, among others, Li Wan, Anna Metcalfe, Chen Bo, Simon Shieh, Jemima Foxtrot, Leila Nashef, Richard Loria, and Gao Xiu'e. I am eternally grateful to them and everyone else who has provided support of any form in my explorations of Chinese literature and literature in general. Finally, I would like to thank Ugly Duckling Presse for their faith in my work and for giving a relatively unknown translator the chance to publish their first passion project.

TRANSLATOR'S NOTE

It seems to me that one of the most difficult aspects of translating Chinese poetry, and I suppose poetry of any language, is capturing the voice of the original. The Chinese language is structured very differently to English, which means that what comes out the other end is often far from a word-for-word translation. Although the general meaning can be relatively easily preserved in most cases (with some important exceptions!) it can be challenging to reproduce how a certain turn of phrase *feels*. My constant fear when translating poetry is that while I may be able to get across what is being said, I might leave behind the voice that is saying it.

This concern seems particularly pertinent to the poetry of Ma Yan, whose authorial presence suffuses her writing. Its intimate tone and emotional reach—from invigoratingly buoyant to evocatively melancholic—are some of the qualities that first drew me to her poems. It has always been at the back of my mind as I've attempted to translate her work, and it has informed how I've made certain decisions.

One example is "Jokes, Irony, Mockery, and Deeper Significances", which ends with a crude description of giving birth: "I spread my legs and grab / my son's head, drag him out, stretch him out big." In Chinese, "stretch him out big" (把他拉扯大) means to bring up a child in adverse circumstances, a meaning that is utterly lost in my translation. I considered using an English expression that captured some of this sense (like "bring him up through thick and thin"), but in the end the editors at UDP—Sarah, chuck, and Michael—and I settled for the literal translation because of the physicality of the image in the context of what precedes it. No doubt Ma Yan had both the literal and general meaning in mind when she wrote this line, but this is one of many instances where a choice had to be made—a choice based on an attempt to remain true to what I perceive to be her poetic voice.

Another challenge I faced was Ma Yan's range of registers, from the terse grammar of classical Chinese to the colloquial expressions of the Sichuanese dialect (Sichuan being the province where she was born and grew up), as well as a kind of intimate colloquialism that can inspire in the reader a guilty sense of intruding upon a private conversation. My decisions in these instances are usually based upon a notion of correspondence to English-language culture. For example, when Ma Yan writes "诡诡" in "Flirting (Teasing Out Feeling)", an archaic term that refers to argumentative sophistry, I write "reductio ad absurdum," hoping that the role of Latin in the English-language world corresponds to a certain extent to the role of classical Chinese in modern China. Similarly, with "油爆得很嘎！", which bursts out of the page in "Just Take it Easy" in coarse Sichuanese slang to describe the oiliness of cured meat in terms often applied to lecherous old men, I put "They're greasy old buggers!" which seems to approach the shift in tone that appears in the original. Decisions such as these often seem imperfect, only rough approximations of a feast of cultural signification immediately available to the Chinese reader. Unfortunately, I know of no better way to deal with these isolated instances.

Ma Yan is clearly a poet who is interested in the possibilities of language. In "To Everyone's Demons and Angels", a character (presumably Kang He, to whom the poem is dedicated) quotes a line from Confucius' Analects, "觚不觚。觚哉！觚哉！" in which Confucius expresses displeasure that he has not been served wine in a vessel proper to the occasion—namely, a *gu* (觚). I have translated this as: "This *gu*'s no *gu*. Where's the *gu*? Where's the *gu*?" but it doesn't quite capture the grammatical structure of the original. It is notoriously difficult to render classical Chinese in English, but perhaps a more direct translation of the first half of this quote would be, "The *gu* is not *gu*-ing," which is to say that the *gu* in which Confucius' wine has been served is failing to live up to the basic requirements of being a *gu*: "This so-called *gu* you have presented me with isn't worthy of the name!" This way of writing, in which the same Chinese character can slip seamlessly from noun to verb to adjective to adverb, is almost as alien to contemporary Chinese speakers as it is to English speakers (Confucius was around more than two thousand years ago), and it seems to me that its inclusion in this poem is a result of this linguistic strangeness. As is so often the case with Ma Yan, it is also a glimpse into an interpersonal world of which the reader is not a part; an interest in language shared by Ma Yan and her friend Kang He, revealed in this comical and imperious interjection from one of the towering figures of China's cultural history and in which more than half of the characters are the archaic term *gu*. It's always difficult to know how to translate lines like these, but my final decision is an attempt to walk the line between intelligibility and preserving the sense of the original.

Individual examples of translation difficulties such as those I have given above tend to focus on the intricacies of language, but in this case I do not believe they give a good impression of what it is really *like* to read Ma Yan's work. Perhaps it is worth noting here a little of the literary environment in which she wrote, and particularly an anxiety I have heard voiced by some contemporary Chinese writers about standard Mandarin.

Chinese vernacular poetry began in earnest in the early twentieth century, a period of great political energy that followed the dissolution of the Qing, China's last imperial dynasty, and would culminate in 1949 with the Communist party taking power. The vernacular literature movement was a response to the previously dominant classical literary style, which was difficult for most ordinary Chinese people to understand. It was a movement driven by democratic ideals and took place alongside an attempt to universalize standard Mandarin (based on the Beijing dialect) as a lingua franca within China, an important goal for a nation trying to unite its population in the face of colonial aggression. As a result, the move from classical to vernacular Chinese as the language of literature was accompanied by the standardization of the vernacular, whereby the particularities of different dialects were ironed out in favor of increased communicability. Some feel that this led to a neutered form of written language that lacked the rich literary history of classical Chinese. The cultural policies of Maoist China, depending on who you talk to, were a further assault on the expressive potential of language. In the late 1970s, China began to turn away from Maoism and contemporary Chinese literature as we know it was born, but writers found that the language that was left to them was impoverished. The task for poets and novelists since then has been to expand the scope of linguistic expression through their work, by recreating the Chinese language one book at a time.

Whether or not this narrative is an accurate portrayal of the evolution of vernacular language in twentieth-century China, the anxiety about the insufficiency of standard Mandarin is present among certain contemporary writers. (Though I suspect that anxieties about the insufficiency of language are not limited to those who write in Chinese.) As such, there has been a more or less conscious effort by some poets, particularly those in academic environments, to adopt a range of registers and a complex imagistic symbolism as a means of broadening what they see as the narrow confines of standard vernacular Chinese, and for many of them this is a political as well as aesthetic project.

Ma Yan, therefore, is not alone in her playful use of language, which includes an unrestrained and vibrant use of imagery as well as a blending of literary styles, and in a sense she is a product of the poetic environment of the university in which she honed her craft. However, whereas with many contemporary Chinese writers this practice can sometimes come across as a detached exercise in formal experimentation, there is a sense of emotional *urgency* to Ma Yan's work, a critical need to address something, which undergirds the linguistic play and lends it a vital spontaneity. Nothing about Ma Yan's poetry seems forced. Rather, language seems to be unfolding naturally and freely within the breadth of its expressive potential, in order to confront what must be confronted. Ma Yan is thus concerned with a different set of political and social issues than those addressed by more formally oriented poets. As well as embodying a spirit of playfulness, her poetry is committed to certain realities that it cannot discard—our personal interactions; mental health; the raw experience of existence and co-existence; gender and femininity. I do not want to dwell too long on Ma Yan's themes here as any attempt on my part to explicate them would pale in comparison to her own words. Rather, I hope to convey something about the quality of her writing that I have struggled with as a translator: an ecstatic freedom of thought that is nonetheless chained to certain insurmountable issues to which it cannot help but return. This perhaps gets closer to the main challenge I faced in translating her work, more so than the singular examples of difficult-to-translate expressions I gave above. It is harder to explain the spirit of a writer's work in a translator's note but in the case of Ma Yan it is perhaps one of the most striking facets of her poetry and one of the main reasons I wanted to translate it. I can only hope I'm able to convey some of this quality in this book.

— Stephen Nashef, June 2021

ENDNOTES

THE SELF'S ART OF ILLUSION
"It passeth like this" (my translation) is a quote from the "Zi Han" chapter of the *Analects* of Confucius. Confucius makes this statement standing by the banks of a river, apparently reflecting on time.

SAXIFRAGE
Saxifrage appears in the twentieth-century novel by Shen Congwen, *Border Town*, where it acts as a metaphor for the simple devotion of a young country girl waiting in vain for the return of the man she loves. It has since come to be seen as a romantic symbol for pure and innocent love.

THIS WARMTH HAS NO SOURCE
The line "The reeds that sway also leisurely / disarrange" is a reference to Xu Zhimo's *Taking Leave of Cambridge Again*: "The reeds in the soft mud / Sway leisurely underwater" (my translation).

STUDY
In Chinese the common fig is known as *wuhuaguo* (无花果), which literally means "flowerless fruit," with "fruit" having both its botanical and figurative meaning (i.e., "the fruits of one's labor"). This is not the only time Ma Yan makes use of this wordplay (see "Suffering Does not Destroy What Makes Suffering Possible", where I have chosen to translate it differently).

TO EVERYONE'S DEMONS AND ANGELS
"This *gu*'s no *gu*. Where's the *gu*? Where's the *gu*?" is a not

particularly famous Confucius quote, where *gu* refers to a goblet for drinking wine. A displeased Confucius, who was somewhat of a stickler for the rules of etiquette, reportedly said this at a meal when the vessel of wine with which he was presented did not meet the proper standards for a *gu*.

THE LOVE OF LITTLE GIRLS
"Life is sweet and… life is sweet" are lines that appear in the 1998 film *Eternity and a Day*, the title of which is the epigraph of the poem, "Fine Snow".

FINE SNOW
The narrow alleys in the older areas of some of China's northern cities, particularly Beijing, are referred to as *hutongs*.

THE WORLD RAINS A NIGHT
Zhongguancun is an area in Beijing, not far from the university Ma Yan attended.

KNOCKING PERSIMMONS IN AUTUMN
"Knocking persimmons" refers to the practice of striking a persimmon tree with bamboo sticks so that the fruit falls from the branches and can be collected.

FLIRTING (TEASING OUT FEELING)
In Chinese the word for the verb "flirt" is composed of two characters, *tiao* (调) to tease or provoke, and *qing* (情) meaning sentiment or feeling. Because of the poem's wordplay I use both "flirt" and "teasing out feeling" to translate what appears in the original Chinese as just one word: *tiaoqing*.

A TEAHOUSE ON A RAINY DAY (OR LION ROCK)

There are many Lion Rocks in China, but here Ma Yan is likely referring to the area of Chengdu.

In China, "hair-washing girl" can be a euphemism for sex worker.

EXTRAVAGANZA

In the epigraph Ma Yan writes "virtue has another meaning: to slash." This is a reference to the homophonic characters *yi* (义), meaning virtue, and *yi* (刈), meaning to slash or to scythe.

SMALL IS SMALL

The heroic little sisters were two sisters from Inner Mongolia, Longmei and Yurong, who became famous in 1964 at the ages of twelve and nine years old when they risked their lives to save a flock of sheep during a freak snowstorm. Longmei lost her left thumb and Yurong lost both her feet to frostbite.

SMOOTH TALKER

Ma Yan's original term for what I have translated as "heart-shattering potion" is *duanchangsan* (断肠散), which is a mythical poison that appears in the martial arts novel *Eight Parts of the Sky Dragon*. It literally translates to something like "gut-fracturing powder," but a fractured gut is also often used to describe the sensation of heartbreak.

Ma Yan 马雁 was born in 1979 to Chinese Muslim parents in Chengdu and went on to study classical Chinese literature at Peking University, where she began writing the poems for which she would later be known. An active participant in the Peking University poetry scene, she returned to Chengdu in 2003 to help take care of her father who was ill. She continued to write poetry, prose, and criticism that she posted on her blog, much of which has since been collected and published in book form. She only released two self-published collections of poetry before taking her own life in 2010, but her work has seen a sharp rise in popularity in the decade since her death and continues to influence a new generation of young Chinese writers. *I Name Him Me* is her first book to be published in English.